A guide to collecting and analysing information for a Prospective Adopter's Report (formerly Form F) England

Elaine Dibben

Published by
British Association for Adoption & Fostering
(BAAF)
Saffron House
6–10 Kirby Street
London EC1N 8TS
www.baaf.org.uk

Charity registration 275689 (England and Wales) and SC039337 (Scotland)

© BAAF 2010

British Library Cataloguing in Publication Data
A catalogue record for this book is available from the British Library

ISBN 978 1 905664 40 5

Project management by Shaila Shah, Director of Publications, BAAF
Designed and typeset by Helen Joubert Design Ltd
Printed in Great Britain by The Lavenham Press

BAAF is the leading UK-wide membership organisation for all those concerned
with adoption, fostering and child care issues

Contents

Acknowledgements

My main acknowledgement must be to Roger Chapman, whose guide, *Undertaking Fostering Assessments,* established the successful format for this series. Although the focus of this book is adoption assessments, I have retained relevant sections and adapted some of the useful checklists and questions that are relevant to both types of assessments.

I am also grateful to Chris Christophides, Fran Moffat and Mo O'Reilly for their helpful comments and encouragement and Shaila Shah for her confidence in me bringing this book to fruition.

I would also like to thank social worker colleagues whom I have consulted including Buckinghamshire County Council who allowed me to adapt their information on second opinion reports, Solihull Metropolitan Borough Council who allowed me to use and adapt their pet questionnaire and Lesley Newth West for sharing her insights from practice.

The author

Elaine Dibben started her social work career in residential social work and qualified in 1988. She has over 20 years' experience of working in adoption and fostering in local authority and voluntary agency settings and is a strong advocate for the importance of securing permanence in family settings for children who cannot return to their parents' care.

She joined BAAF in 2004 to become manager of the Independent Review Mechanism, which she set up and ran until 2009, when she moved to take on a wider role in BAAF as a trainer/consultant. She is currently a Fostering and Adoption Development Consultant for BAAF alongside acting as a panel chair for both adoption and fostering panels.

She lives in Oxfordshire with her husband Steve.

Introduction

This guide is designed to help social workers to conduct a comprehensive assessment of prospective adopters. It is to be used by assessing social workers to complete a prospective adopter's report using the BAAF Prospective Adopter's Report (formerly Form F) England, which meets the requirements set out in the Adoption Agencies Regulations 2005 Part 4; Schedule 4, Part 1 and in both statutory and practice guidance.

The guide is primarily based on Section B of the Prospective Adopter's Report (PAR), which is the descriptive part which brings together information about the applicant – what has made them into the person they are today and what creates the stability and security in their adult life that would enable them to become an adopter. The information covers the applicant as an individual, their family, and wider environmental factors.

It is expected that assessing social workers will be familiar with the PAR. However, below is a brief overview of Sections A to E of the PAR.

A brief overview of Sections A to E of the BAAF Prospective Adopter's Report

Section A

Section A covers factual information about the application and the applicants. On page 1, there is reference to whether a full or brief report has been prepared. In Appendix 3 of this guide, there are some suggestions on what should be included in a brief report.

Section B

Section B, which is the descriptive part of the report, is covered in detail in this guide.

Section C

Section C brings together the different reports, references and other supporting materials. C11, which covers observations on other members of the household, and C12, which is a summary of information and evaluations from referee visits, are included at the end of the document so they can be treated as confidential where required. Other reports that could be included in this section include references from ex-partners, additional references, where there are children in the household, those from health visitors, nurseries or schools or employment references, particularly where a prospective adopter is or has been employed in a child care capacity. All third party information should be treated as confidential and not shared with the applicants without the express permission of the referees.

Section D

This section can be used by the assessing agency as a checklist to ensure that all references and statutory checks have been completed. It contains personal and confidential information and data about the applicants; the section on verification of checks is expected to have a limited circulation. Whilst it can be presented as part of panel papers at the point of approval, and to the Department for Education, if required, for intercountry adoption applications, it does not need to be included with forms sent out to other agencies.

Section E

Section E sets out the BAAF adoption competencies, which list the skills and knowledge needed by prospective adopters, and allows the assessing social worker to indicate whether the competency has been evidenced during the assessment. It then provides space to set out how any gaps in knowledge or experience will be addressed in an action plan. It is for agencies to decide how or whether they make use of this section, as it is not required by regulation.

What this guide is

This guide primarily takes Section B of the BAAF Prospective Adopter's Report and breaks down each area for exploration, with the applicants, into four parts:

● a list of questions that can be asked of applicants or can be used to facilitate further discussion in order to collect some of the basic information required for the purposes of the assessment;

● where appropriate, extracts from the relevant section from the Guidance Notes which accompany the BAAF PAR or relevant guidance from the DCSF *Practice Guidance on Preparing and Supporting Adopters*;

● some suggestions for how the information that has been collected can be analysed to see if it will be positive for adoption or could be seen as a potential area of concern or vulnerability by the assessing social worker;

- examples of how the information given could be evidenced from sources both within and outside of the family to provide verification of their account.

It is hoped that, by making use of this guide, assessing social workers will be able to collect the information which will form the basis of a sound assessment. It will also help to identify those areas where there is a need for support or further training and these can then be addressed in the final column of the BAAF Competencies in Section E, where this is being used.

Having collected the information, the guide places an emphasis on the analysis of the information collected. This is an area of concern which has been identified in some of the cases presented to the Independent Review Mechanism[1] panels. Where applicants have been encouraged to write their own accounts relating to sections of the PAR, it is important that this information is not reproduced in its entirety but edited by the assessing social worker to provide the key information required. The social worker will then need to analyse this information alongside other information in the report.

It is also intended that this guide may help in the planning of sessions with applicants and there is a helpful timesheet in Appendix 1, which can be used by the assessor alone or in conjunction with their supervisor, to plan out the course of the assessment process and agree in what order areas will be covered and within what timescale. It can be helpful for the social worker to agree a contract with the applicants at the beginning of the assessment setting out expectations e.g. the number of anticipated visits, whether these will be held in the applicant's home or in the office, how any differences between the assessing social worker and applicant will be managed, and whether there will be a halfway meeting or second opinion visit.

Some thought should be given to the order in which these subjects are covered with the applicants, as it may be more appropriate to cover more personal and sometimes painful areas of their lives once a relationship between you – the assessor and the applicant – has been established.

Where adoption agencies are using Attachment Style interviews or Adult Attachment interviews, the information from these interviews will inform the assessment and may highlight other areas needing further exploration during the assessment.

The guide also divides the questions into three parts:

1. individual profile and family and environmental factors;

2. present circumstances;

3. becoming adopter/s – the assessment of adoptive parenting capacity.

These headings broadly mirror those used to introduce the different parts of Section B of the PAR, and the questions fall into these categories. This may help to give some structure to the assessment task and some focus as to the order in which the various topics may be covered by the assessor.

---

[1] http://www.dcsf.gov.uk/everychildmatters/_download/?id=6603

The information in Chapters 4, 5 and the Appendices is intended to complement each agency's own procedures and formats for these areas. These include the following.

- A plan for an interview with a personal referee for an applicant.

- Suggestions of areas to cover for a health and safety check of the applicant's home.

- A proforma for a pet assessment.

- Areas to be covered by a safer caring policy.

- An example of an ecomap showing where applicants get their support from.

- Suggestions for additional areas to cover when considering applications for specific children/intercountry adoption.

- Information to be covered in brief reports.

- Information to be covered in second opinion visits.

In this guide, the term "applicant" is more commonly used to obviate the necessity of continuously using the terms "applicant/applicants".

What this guide is not

This guide is **not** intended to be a quick and easy way of undertaking an assessment. It offers a way of collecting the basic information needed to complete the process. Although most of the guide is presented in question format, it is not intended that the questions merely be fired at the applicant. Rather, they are designed to help the assessor cover key areas in what should be a dynamic process rather than one which consists merely of answers to questions or the completion of a checklist. It is hoped they will also stimulate ideas for the assessing social worker for questions that are pertinent to each individual assessment.

Assessors must be alert to the idiosyncrasies and complexities of each different applicant they assess and be prepared to pursue different lines of questioning and exploration accordingly and analyse that information on the basis of its relevance to the adoptive parent role.

The guide is also not designed to lead to any standardisation of assessments. It is important for assessors to maintain their individual styles of seeking, analysing and presenting information.

This guide should be seen as a tool to help in the assessment process and not an end in itself.

Individual profile and family and environmental factors

The issues for consideration listed below cover the applicant's family of origin; other significant relationships including relationships with previous partners; identity issues; education; employment; health and leisure activities; and other relevant information including personal characteristics and issues with regards to childlessness, if appropriate.

Guidance Notes to PAR

It is suggested that during the assessment the social worker should ask for specific descriptions and pay particular attention to the applicant's quality of their relationship with their mother and father. Supplementary questions should ask for the applicant's memories of specific events that back up any global descriptions if these are not given spontaneously. These should be followed by specific questions about any experiences of rejection, upset, illness or hurt as well as loss, any abuse or separation experienced by the applicant and their memories of the way that their parent/s responded to this.

In addition, applicants should be asked for their own explanations of why their parents behaved in the way that they did. They should also be asked for their views on the influence of their childhood experiences on the formation of their adult personality.

Family of origin

- Compile a genogram/family tree. (Include dates of birth and whether family members are living or deceased.) Although this could be completed by the applicant prior to this session, it is more useful to complete a genogram jointly with the applicant and revisit it during subsequent visits, as you will find that this can be a useful visual tool to help people talk through their family background and history including areas such as health, ethnicity and cultural diversity. The final genogram is to be included in Section C of the PAR.

- Where were you born and brought up?

- Describe your mother and the nature of your relationship with her. If you had to choose five words to illustrate this, which ones would they be? Can you recall any examples to evidence the words you have chosen? Did the nature of your relationship with your mother change at all during your childhood?

- Describe your father and the nature of your relationship with him. If you had to choose five words to illustrate this, which ones would they be? Can you recall any examples to evidence the words you have chosen? Did the relationship change at all during your childhood?

- If either of your parents were not present for some or all of your childhood, how did this affect you as a child?

- Give details of any other significant people who were involved in your care during your childhood and your relationship with them.

- As a child, who did you feel closest to and why?

- Describe your relationship with your siblings and any specific role you or they played in that relationship. How has this relationship changed in adulthood?

- What good things do you remember about your childhood?

- What unhappy memories or times do you remember (e.g. experiences of rejection, upset, illness or hurt)? Was there anyone that helped you at that time?

- How would you describe your overall experience of early childhood (i.e. pre-adolescence)?

- What are your significant memories of your teenage years?

- What was your overall experience of adolescence?

- Was adolescence a time of experimentation for you?

- How have your experiences as a child shaped the person you are today?

- In which ways are you like your parents and how are you different?

- How were you affected by any experiences of separation, loss or bereavement during your childhood? How were these dealt with at the time and who supported you through those times? What has been their impact on you as an adult?

- What are your memories of special occasions (birthdays, religious festivals, holidays)?

- If you were adopted, how did your parents tell you about being adopted and what was your understanding of the circumstances of your adoption?

- Were you aware of anyone in your family or friendship circle who was adopted or fostered? Were you aware of any issues arising from that experience?

- What was your overall experience of being parented at the time and on reflection?

- What was your experience of religion in your family upbringing? Is this something you have continued in your life?

- How do you view your culture and how is this reflected in your upbringing and life now?

- What have been the significant events in your adult life?

- What has given you the greatest satisfaction in your life so far and what has been the biggest disappointment?

- How would you describe yourself now?

- What do you feel are your strengths and weaknesses?

- How might others describe you?

DCSF Practice Guidance on Preparing and Assessing Prospective Adopters

- Practitioners should assess whether the prospective adopter's account of childhood is balanced with both positive and negative aspects.

- Can the prospective adopter give examples to illustrate any generalisations about their relationships with their parents?

ASSESSOR'S ANALYSIS

- In analysing this information, it will be important to acknowledge and be sensitive to different styles and models of parenting in families because of cultural influences.

- What experiences from their background does the applicant bring to adoption e.g. benefits from a happy, stable background, experience of inconsistent or poor parenting, experience of loss, separation or feeling different? Illustrate with some examples.

- What is the applicant's experience of attachment to their parents/ caregivers?

- Where the applicant has provided negative information about their childhood or family relationships, what evidence is there that they have been able to overcome the impact of these?

- **Has the applicant been able to give a coherent account of their past?**

- **Is the applicant able to be reflective?**

- **What evidence is there of insight into how the applicant's past has affected them as adults today?**

- **What evidence is there of their resilience and ability to deal with difficulties?**

- **What are the contra-indications or potential areas of vulnerability for them adopting a child and how could these risks be minimised or gaps filled?**

Verify through:

- Personal and family member references, ensuring that referees are sought who have knowledge of particular times/periods of the applicant's childhood or relationships

- Interview with partner including asking about their view of applicant's personality

- If applicable, a reference from a counsellor/therapist

Other significant relationships (excluding previous partners)

- Who was the relationship with?

- At what stage of your life was this?

- What was the nature of the relationship?

- What effect has the relationship had on you?

- Is the relationship still ongoing?

- If it has ended, how did it end and what was the effect of this on you?

Relationships with previous partners

For each partnership

- Who was the relationship with?

- How long did it last and when did it start and finish?

- What was the status of the relationship?

- Why did the relationship end?

- Were there children in or from the relationship?

- With whom did the children live after the relationship ended and how was this decided?

- How were the children affected by the breakup of the relationship?

- How did you help them deal with this?

- What contact is there now with your ex-partner and any children?

- If contact for the children is, or was involved, how has this been managed?

- If children from a previous relationship visit or stay over, is there sufficient physical space in the home?

- What is the attitude of these children and their other parent to this adoption application?

- How much have they been told / included in discussions about the proposed adoption?

- How will these children's needs continue to be met, alongside those of the child/ren placed?

- What impact might these relationships have on a child/ren placed for adoption?

- What have you learned from the relationship/s?

- Can we contact your ex-partner for a reference?

- If not, what are the reasons for this?

- If this is not possible, are there referees who knew you when you were in that relationship and who could be contacted?

NB: If a decision is taken not to make contact with an ex-partner, the social worker will need to detail the reasons for this. If an ex-partner does not respond to requests for a reference, you will need to state what efforts were made to try to obtain the reference.

DCSF Practice Guidance on Preparing and Assessing Prospective Adopters

Key information may also come from former partners who have jointly parented or cared for a child with the prospective adopter, such as a former spouse, civil partner or person they have lived with, in an enduring family relationship. Where the prospective adopter has jointly parented or cared for a child with a former partner, the agency should approach the former partner unless the agency considers there are exceptional reasons for not doing so.

Where the agency is contemplating approaching former partners, it should remind the prospective adopter why this is being done and explain how the information will be sought and how it is carefully considered, forming one element of a multi-faceted assessment.

> It is important to scrutinise the patterns and qualities of the applicant's previous relationships.
>
> Can they demonstrate exclusive and stable relationships that can provide environments of nurture and permanence for children placed? The same degree of enquiry is needed irrespective of marital status or sexuality.

ASSESSOR'S ANALYSIS

- Is there corroboration of the details of any previous relationship from the ex-partner or a referee who knew the applicant and the ex-partner when they were together?

- If there are children from a previous relationship, what is the evidence that their needs have been fully considered in this application?

- Can any experience of managing/maintaining contact with their own children or stepchildren be helpful in terms of thinking about attitudes to openness in adoption and contact for adopted children?

- What evidence is there that the current relationship (if there is one) is more likely to be stable and satisfying than the previous one?

- Are there any patterns emerging from previous relationships or from how they ended?

- Are there any potential areas of vulnerability identified for the applicant in relation to their plans to adopt?

- Are there any issues arising from any other significant relationships the applicant has had that might have a bearing on this application?

NB: Where areas of risk have been identified in relation to ex-partners or other family members, a risk assessment should be considered.

Verify through:

- References from ex-partners, essential where there were children in or of the relationship, unless issues of risk are identified

- Personal and family member references, particularly important if an ex-partner is not being or cannot be sought to obtain verification of the account of the relationship

Identity

Guidance Notes to PAR

Identity includes those factors associated with class, ethnicity, gender, sexuality, culture, language and spirituality.

As well as assessing the issues that give the applicant their own sense of identity, it is important to provide information on and assess the applicant's attitudes to diversity that may be relevant to their care of a child.

- What do you think are some of the components that make up your own sense of identity or describe who you are?

- How would you describe your own identity (i.e. in terms of your gender, language, ethnicity, disability, class, culture, sexuality and spirituality)?

- Do you know where your name originates from or why it was chosen for you?

- What do you know about your family history?

- How do you view Britain today in terms of the mix of different ethnic, cultural and religious groups within the population?

- What is the ethnic mix of your own local area?

- Does your lifestyle reflect the fact that we live in a multiracial/multicultural society (i.e. food, music, friends, art/ornaments, etc)?

- Do you follow any particular faith? If so, how important is this to you and how is this incorporated into your lifestyle?

- Have you ever experienced any prejudice or bullying?

- Can you give some examples of reasons people might be discriminated against in society?

- How did your parents and extended family relate to people from different ethnic and religious backgrounds or people who were disabled or gay or lesbian?

- What contact do you have, or have you had, socially or through work with people of other ethnicities, people who are disabled or gay or lesbian?

- How has this affected your own attitudes and values?

- (For applicants with children) How have you raised your children in relation to these issues? Give examples of how you have discussed these matters with them (there may be examples of issues raised on TV or by friends and people in your network or situations they have experienced at school).

DCSF Practice Guidance on Preparing and Assessing Prospective Adopters

To help the prospective adopter gain an insight into the significance of the child's sense of identity, they should be encouraged to reflect on the development of their own identity.

Prospective adopters, who are considering adopting children from a different ethnic or racial background to their own, need to consider the effect on the child. They need to demonstrate an awareness of the value of promoting self-esteem, providing knowledge and understanding of the child's background and proactively challenging discrimination.

ASSESSOR'S ANALYSIS

- Is there evidence that the applicant has non-discriminatory attitudes and values?

- Has the applicant had any personal experience that might help them care for a child from a different ethnicity, or a disabled child?

- Are there people in their family and friends network who could help the applicant if they were adopting a child from a different cultural, ethnic or religious background?

- Were there family members with discriminatory attitudes? And if so, has the applicant given thought to how they would deal with this and is the assessor satisfied that this will not expose children to negative experiences?

- Does the assessor feel confident that this is a family which would challenge prejudice in an appropriate way if it arose?

Verify through:

- Personal references

- Feedback from preparation training

- Ecomap (evidence of levels of contact and support)

Education

Some of the factual information gathered here will be included in the chronology in C3 and does not need to be repeated in the main report. For applicants who attended schools in other countries, you will need to ascertain the structure of the education system that was in place.

- Which schools did you attend?

- What type of schools did you attend e.g. state schools, faith schools, grammar schools or private schools? Did this impact on you in any way?

- What was your experience of junior/secondary schooling?

- Did you experience any additional changes in schooling? How was this managed?

- What was the attitude of your parents towards your education? Were they actively involved in your schooling? Was this different to any of your siblings?

- What qualifications did you gain?

- What was your experience of further/higher education?

- Have you gained any qualifications/skills as an adult? Do you have any plans to undertake further training or qualifications?

- What is your attitude to education and training now as a parent/prospective adopter?

- For applicants with children, what has your experience been, as a parent, with the education system?

DCSF Practice Guidance on Preparing and Assessing Prospective Adopters

A history of the prospective adopter's education will be needed, from pre-school to higher or further education.

The prospective adopter will usually have clear views about the value of their education and its influence on their life. The practitioner should assess whether the prospective adopter is likely to help a child achieve their full potential, rather than expect the child to fulfil a particular set of expectations.

ASSESSOR'S ANALYSIS

- **From their own experience of education, how will the applicant promote the education and learning opportunities for adopted children?**

- **What importance does the applicant place on academic achievement as opposed to a wider view of development and achievement?**

- **Will the applicant be confident in liaising with schools to obtain a place or advocate for any additional educational support needed by an adopted child?**

- **Are there any areas where the agency might need to offer support or training?**

Verify through:

- **Checking certificates of qualifications**

- **Written reference from school if applicant has a child currently attending nursery/school**

- **Asking applicant to contribute a written piece towards the assessment**

Employment

Some of the factual information gathered here will be included in the chronology in C3 and does not need to be repeated in the main report.

- Give details of your experience of work from leaving school to the present day (pay particular attention to work involving children or in a care situation) and explain any gaps in employment.

- What opportunities have you had for training in your employment?

- How have you benefited from these?

- What was your parents' attitude to work?

- What are your ambitions/plans for the future with regard to work?

- How important is work to you?

- Do you plan to vary or leave work when a child is placed? How will this affect your lifestyle, support networks, etc?

- If you are intending to work, what plans do you have for covering child care during school holidays or when a child is ill?

- What discussions have you had as a couple about making changes in one or both of your working lives and how was this decided (where applicable)?

- How will your work commitments fit with your role as an adoptive parent? Have you discussed this with your employer? Are you are aware of your employer's policies on statutory adoption leave and statutory adoption pay and do you intend to make use of these entitlements?

DCSF Practice Guidance on Preparing and Assessing Prospective Adopters

Balancing work commitments with parenting a child placed for adoption is a key consideration for prospective adopters. Their assessment should look at their work patterns and how these may need to change after the placement. Prospective adopters should be encouraged to use their rights to statutory adoption leave and pay during the initial stages of a placement.

...A systematic picture of the care a child may need and the challenges presented ... may help the practitioner and the prospective adopter to decide whether their work patterns could fit with the needs of a child.

Where the prospective adopters are a couple, it may be difficult to decide whose work patterns should change most if equal adjustments are not feasible. They should be encouraged to plan an arrangement that is most likely to meet the needs of a child placed for adoption and their own work commitments.

ASSESSOR'S ANALYSIS

- Are there any issues arising from the applicant's pattern of employment, e.g. evidence of stability, job security, inconsistencies or unexplained gaps in employment?

- Are there skills or experiences from the applicant's employment that would be relevant to their suitability to adopt?

- Has the applicant undertaken any work based on professional qualifications that evidence positive attitudes towards training and personal/professional development?

- How flexible is the applicant in terms of fitting work around the needs of a child placed for adoption? Where there is no full-time carer proposed, are the plans they have proposed to cover child care during school holidays or when a child is ill realistic and likely to be in a child's best interests?

Verify through:

- Current employer's reference (or if self employed, through references from clients or accountant as appropriate)

- Any previous employers' references if involved in child care or other care settings

- References from people in support network, particularly if they may be involved in support arrangements

- Written details of adoption pay and leave scheme offered by employer

Health

Please also refer to section C6 of the PAR where details of the medical adviser's summary on the health of the applicant should be recorded.

- What efforts do you make to try to maintain a good level of health?

- What physical activities do you do to maintain a healthy lifestyle?

- What is your attitude towards and your experience of smoking, drug or alcohol use?

- Do you or any member of your family have a disability? If so, how does that impact on your/their life? Are there any health issues arising from this? How would this impact on your ability to parent a child?

- Where a medical has indicated that your weight or possible obesity may be an issue, what efforts are you making to change your lifestyle and lose weight?

- Do you now, or have you in the past, suffered from any significant illnesses including any mental health or stress-related difficulties? Are you taking any medication regularly? Is this reviewed by a medical practitioner?

- If so, please give details and any ways in which this may affect your ability to care for a child.

- What support do you have from other people to help you manage any ongoing health issues, including health professionals?

- Do you feel you are an emotionally strong person? How have you managed and responded to stressful episodes in your life?

- Do you understand how physical or mental health issues can play a part in children needing to be looked after?

- Do any children or other adults in the household have any health issues which could impact on you or an adopted child?

- Are there any other family members not living in the household who have any health issues which could impact on you or an adopted child?

DCSF Practice Guidance on Preparing and Assessing Prospective Adopters

Health is a key and complex factor in assessing whether a prospective adopter has the capacity and potential longevity to care for a child into adulthood. If a prospective adopter has particular health problems, these need to be identified and assessed by a medical practitioner so that the effect on their capacity to care for and parent a child can be considered as fully as possible.

Where a couple are applying to adopt, they may be unaware of their partner's health history. Such information remains confidential to the person it is about and should not be shared with their partner unless the prospective adopter gives their written permission.

Where a member of a couple has not shared significant health-related information with their partner, the practitioner should discuss this with them on a one-to-one basis to explore their reasons. Support should be offered and the prospective adopter encouraged to share such information with their partner. If they still remain reluctant to do so, this raises questions about the degree of openness in their relationship.

ASSESSOR'S ANALYSIS

- In reaching conclusions about the implications of health issues on the application, the social worker needs to take account of the comments of both the GP and agency medical adviser.

- Does the applicant have any physical or mental health difficulties that would impact on their ability to adopt a child?

- What support do they have in place to help them manage any existing conditions?

- Where the medical adviser has indicated the applicant is overweight, have they made efforts to change their diet and lifestyle in a way which will be sustained?

- Where the applicant is taking anti-depressants and this is supported by their GP and the medical adviser, what evidence is there of their ability to manage stressful situations?

- Are there any health considerations for any other family members that would impact on the applicant's availability and plans to adopt?

- Is there evidence that they seek appropriate medical advice and would also do this for a child placed?

- Is there any evidence that they could be over-anxious about their health or that of a child placed? If so, how will this be managed?

Verify through:

- Medical references, including from consultants and counsellors where identified

- Personal references

Leisure and recreational interests

- What interests or hobbies do you enjoy?

- Why are they important to you? When do you do them and with whom?

- How much time is involved in these activities?

- What activities do you do with your partner (where applicable)?

- How would adopting a child affect/fit in with these activities? Which activities would you want to involve them in?

- Do you have any other skills or talents?

ASSESSOR'S ANALYSIS

- **How flexible is the applicant in terms of fitting hobbies or interests around adopting a child?**

- **What interests/talents could they share with a child placed with them?**

- **Do they recognise the value of out of school activities to boost self-esteem for children who have been looked after?**

- **Does the applicant recognise the importance of having time for themselves, individually and, where applicable, as a couple?**

Verify through:

- **Personal references**

- **Certificates/trophies, etc**

Other relevant information

Criminal convictions

- Have you received any cautions or convictions during your childhood or as an adult?

- Can you explain the circumstances that led to the incident and how it was dealt with?

- If you were still living at home, what was the response to the incident from your parents?

- Who else knows about this caution/conviction?

- How do you now reflect on the incident and what changes did you make following the incident?

- How would you explain this to any child placed with you and how would you deal with them if they became involved in any offending behavior?

DCSF Practice Guidance on Preparing and Assessing Prospective Adopters

Where a prospective adopter is found to have committed an offence which is not specified under AAR 23.2 or 23.4, the agency should discuss this with the prospective adopter. It should consider the nature of the offence, the effect on others and the prospective adopter, the penalty applied, date of the offence, and whether or not these factors raise doubts about the safety and welfare of children who might potentially be placed with the prospective adopter. In cases where an enhanced CRB check has led to the disclosure of "soft" information, it will need to be carefully considered.

Where it becomes clear to the agency that information about convictions or cautions has not been shared between partners, it should ask the person with the conviction or caution why this is so. Failure to share such information with a partner should be explored. It is possible that it might indicate a lack of trust and openness in the relationship, especially if they remain reluctant to share such information after they have been counselled by their social worker.

ASSESSOR'S ANALYSIS

- Has the applicant been able to reflect on the incident and accept responsibility for their actions?

- Is there any pattern of incidents which would indicate an area of concern?

- Are there any implications of any offences for the safety and well-being of a child being placed with them?

- How has this been addressed by the adoption agency? Has a manager been consulted about the significance of the offence and its implications for the application? Was a formal risk assessment undertaken?

Verify through:

- **CRB checks and Independent Safeguarding Authority (ISA) registration as applicable**

- **Discussion with partner of applicant, once certain they are aware of incident**

- **Personal references**

Current adult relationship (for those in a partnership being assessed as a couple)

- How, where and when did you meet?

- How did the relationship develop?

- What do you feel makes the relationship successful?

- When did you decide to make a permanent commitment to each other?

- Where do you see yourselves in 20 years' time?

- What qualities do each of you bring to the relationship?

- How much time do you spend together?

- What roles do each of you have in the relationship and in your household? What makes your relationship work?

- How do you make decisions as a couple? Can you give some examples of this?

- Are there differences in how you communicate with each other? Do you find it easy to talk about your feelings or concerns?

- How have you dealt with problems, disagreements, stress, anger, or any infidelity or separations, individually and as a couple?

- How do you support each other at these times?

- Have you ever sought professional help during difficult times in your relationship? If so, from whom and for how long? Was the professional help useful or not?

- What has been the most difficult thing you have been through as a couple and how did you support each other through this? Were there things you would change or have changed as a result of this experience?

- (Where the couple come from different ethnic backgrounds) What have been the positives arising from this? Have there been any issues you have had to address arising from your different backgrounds? Have you experienced any difficulties with your extended families and, if so, have you been able to resolve these?

- How do you show affection to each other, at home and outside the home?

- What do you see as the strengths of your relationship? How has your relationship developed over time?

- Do you think there are any vulnerable areas in your relationship? How might you deal with these?

- How would you describe your partner?

- What are your partner's strengths/weaknesses or things that irritate you about him or her?

- Have you thought about how adopting a child might affect your relationship, thinking about both the positives and any stresses this might create?

- (If the applicant is single) If not in a current relationship, do you envisage having a relationship in the future? If one develops in the future, how would you manage the impact of this on a child placed with you?

- (If applicant is gay or lesbian) How will you explain your relationship to any child placed and help a child to answer questions about this? What experience do you already have of this within your family or circle of friends?

DCSF Practice Guidance on Preparing and Assessing Prospective Adopters

- The practitioner needs to establish whether the relationship is stable enough (steady, balanced and resilient) for both partners to parent a child placed for adoption with them and permanent enough (lasting, constant and enduring) to withstand the stresses of adopting a child.

- Can the partners jointly meet the parenting needs of a child placed for adoption with them?

- In looking at whether a couple's relationship has stability and permanence, the practitioner should explore the history of their relationship, how well it works for them and their commitment to it; whether it has been tested and how it survived; how difficulties and conflicts arise, how they are resolved, and how decisions are made; how both partners support each other and meet each other's emotional needs; how the couple adapt to changing circumstances and remain flexible;

- ... same sex couples should consider how they will explain their sexuality and their relationship to a child placed for adoption with them. They should be able to help the child feel at ease with their own sexuality as they grow through childhood and into adolescence. In some cases, the child may need support to be able to explain this to their friends and peers.

ASSESSOR'S ANALYSIS

- **What is the evidence that this is a stable and secure relationship? How does it differ from any previous relationships?**

- **Is there evidence that this relationship is strong enough to deal with the stress and challenges presented when parenting an adopted child?**

- **Is there evidence of mutual support and understanding of each other's needs?**

- **Are there any areas of vulnerability in the relationship which could be tested by an adopted child? Have these been discussed and have protective factors been identified?**

Verify through:

- **Personal referees who have known both applicants**

- **References from children including adult children living away from home**

- **Marriage/civil partnership certificate (where appropriate)**

The household and its membership

Children in the family

- Give details of any children in the family.

- What is the relationship of the child to each applicant?

- Do any special relationships exist between the children and the applicant?

- Describe the personality and character of each child. Do they have any special needs?

- If there are any disabled children in the family, how do they view their disability and do they have any particular needs which need to be considered?

- If there are any children from a black or minority ethnic background in the family, how do they understand their identity? If any children have a different ethnicity to one of their parents, have there been any issues arising from this and how have they been managed?

- What are their interests and talents?

- How are they doing at nursery/school/college?

- Have they had any input from professionals e.g. CAMHS or other specific services? If so, can we seek a reference from these services?

- If you have any children from previous relationships who live elsewhere, what are the relationships like now between the two sets of children and how has this developed?

- What is their understanding of adoption and why children need to be adopted?

- Do they know any children who are fostered or adopted?

- If any of the children in the household are adopted, what has been their experience of adoption? How will they cope with differences in the circumstances of another child joining the family e.g. different contact arrangements, family backgrounds?

- How did you raise the idea with them of adopting a child?

- How involved have they been in the application process?

- How have you taken account of their views in your decision to adopt? And have these changed over time?

- What do you think will be the benefits for them of an adopted child joining the family?

- What are the areas in which they might be vulnerable? How would you manage these areas?

- What has been their experience of sharing your time/their possessions, etc?

- Do they have other adults outside the immediate family whom they would talk to if they had concerns or were finding things difficult?

- What is the nature of their relationship with any siblings? How might this change if another child/ren joins the family?

Interviews with a child/children

The interviews with the children themselves will be planned according to their age and level of understanding, but could include the following:

- How did your parent/s raise with you the idea of adopting a child/ren?

- What did you feel about this and have your views changed over time?

- Have your parents continued to talk to you about what will be involved from their discussions about adoption during the assessment process?

- Do you know any children who are fostered or adopted?

- Why do you think children may need to be adopted?

- How do you think having another child/ren in the family might affect you?

- What rules are there in your family that a child coming to live here will need to know?

- How could you help an adopted child to settle into your family and neighbourhood?

- What are the good things about living in your family?

- How prepared are you to share with an adopted child (parents' and other family members' time, toys, etc)? Do you do this already with other children?

- How would you feel about an adopted child attending your school?

- What type of child do you think will fit best into your family and why (e.g. age, sex, interests, individual or sibling group)?

- What would you do if you were upset or unhappy about something to do with adoption?

- Are there people whom you would talk to outside of your family?

- Are there any things that worry you about your family adopting a child?

- What do you think will be the good things about adopting a child for you and your family and what might be more difficult?

NB: When working with younger children, it may also be helpful to use other communication methods e.g. drawing/colouring worksheets or picture books or CD Roms to ascertain their views, such as *Bridget's taking a long time* CD Rom by Bridget Betts and Nicky Ball (2004) or *Just a member of the family* by Bridget Betts (2005).

DCSF Practice Guidance on Preparing and Assessing Prospective Adopters

Where other people live in the prospective adopter's household, including their own birth children, adopted children (whether children or adults), or foster children, the prospective adopter should prepare brief profiles of them and their relationships with the prospective adopter. This helps the practitioner to understand the family a child may be joining.

Other people in the household should be given information about adoption so that they may participate in discussions about the consequences of a child being placed for adoption in the family. The practitioner should meet children who are of sufficient age and understanding to ask them for their views and to answer their questions. Generally, the prospective adopter should be told about any issues raised so that they can discuss them with their children.

ASSESSOR'S ANALYSIS

- **How well has the applicant prepared and involved their children for an adopted child joining the family?**

- **Does the applicant have insight into the possible effects (positive and negative) on their existing children of adopting a child?**

- **Has the applicant taken into account the needs and views of their own children when considering the age group/sex of the child they wish to adopt?**

- **How realistic do the children appear to be about the impact of adopting a child?**

- **How resilient do the children appear to be?**

- **Are there areas where the children may be vulnerable and, if so, what action could be taken to minimise this?**

- **Have any concerns been raised by other people involved with the child e.g. extended family members, schools, etc, and how have these been addressed?**

- **Is there evidence that the children have an outlet for expressing any concerns or worries about an adopted child joining the family?**

Other adults in the household

- What is the relationship of any other adult members of your household to you? Are there other significant family members – this could include adult children living away from home – whom you would consider to be part of your household?

- How would you describe them as individuals (personality, employment, experience of children)?

- How much contact do you have with them and when?

- What is their attitude to an adopted child joining the family?

- Are there implications for them if you adopt a child?

- Have you considered what information you will and will not share with these individuals about the child placed with you for adoption?

- How will you ensure that both they, and the child placed with you, will remain safe?

- What role are they likely to play in offering either direct care of the child or more general support?

- Do they have any particular experience, skills or interests that could benefit a child?

- Do they have children who would have contact with any adopted child joining the family?

ASSESSOR'S ANALYSIS

- **Do any other adult members of the household need to be interviewed in relation to this application?**

- **Is there evidence that these people could play a significant role with a child placed in the family?**

- **Could these people be vulnerable in any way and, if so, what action could be taken to minimise this?**

- **Has the applicant grasped the importance of confidentiality but balanced this against keeping other adult members of the household safe?**

Verify through:

- Interviews with birth children and other members of the household

- Personal references

- CRB disclosures on other adults in the household

- References from schools/colleges

Social and support network

Guidance Notes to PAR

Ecomaps are not required in regulation although they can be a powerful tool in representing a person's connection to their social network and the strengths and vulnerabilities associated with this. Combining this with a "timeline" can provide an additional visual and sequential representation of the main events in an applicant's life.

The support network ecomap should be included in Section C2 of the PAR. An example of an ecomap can be found in Chapter 5. It should cover family members, friends and significant professionals involved with the family e.g.GP, priest.

Each entry should include the following:

- Name

- Relationship to applicant

- Ethnicity

- Where they live

- Frequency of contact

- Nature of support offered now and in the future

- What involvement they might have with a child placed and whether they have skills or experience that could be of benefit. (If they will be providing care to the child, consider whether they need a CRB check)

- Age of own children and what role they might play

- Details of any groups/clubs to which the applicant belongs and which provide support.

> ## DCSF Practice Guidance on Preparing and Assessing Prospective Adopters
>
> The prospective adopter's report should set out the views of the wider family and friends towards adoption. If views are negative, how does the prospective adopter intend to respond; if positive, how will this be harnessed to provide support before and after the adoption.
>
> Genograms and ecomaps are useful but alone they do not always give a sufficiently detailed picture of the significance of relatives and friends and their capacity to provide support. These questions, including the quality and nature of potential support, should be explored in detail as part of the assessment.

Support network

- (For single applicants) Who do you see as your main support person, both for yourself and in offering help if you were unable to care for the child placed with you for any reason?

- (For single applicants with a partner) What level of involvement with an adopted child do you envisage your partner having?

- Who do you feel closest to and why? (If this is your partner, who would be next outside of that relationship?)

- Can you recall a recent stressful incident/issue? Who did you confide in and why? How was the matter resolved?

- Do you share all problems with others or do you deal with some on your own?

- Are there any family members or friends who have expressed concerns about you adopting a child? How will you manage this so it does not have a negative impact on you or the child?

- What involvement do you have in local groups or organisations? Are these people aware of your plans to adopt and how do you feel people there would support you?

- Are you aware of the importance of practising safer caring and what might happen if an allegation is made against you?

- Have you thought about what information you would share with your family, friends and neighbours about a child placed with you for adoption?

- How would you ensure that the child remains safe in your network of family, friends and acquaintances and that they, in turn, remain safe from allegations?

- What support would you want to receive from your adoption agency and the social worker for the child (if different) when a child is placed with you?

- What contact do you have with any other adopters? Do you envisage using support groups for adopters before and after a child is placed with you?

- Are you aware of national organisations such as BAAF and Adoption UK which can offer independent, external advice and support? Have you had any involvement with them?

DCSF Practice Guidance on Preparing and Assessing Prospective Adopters

The practitioner should try to establish the extent of the prospective adopter's integration or isolation within their community. Do they share any interests with local people or participate in local events or social activities? Local people provide friendships and social acceptance. Such relationships could change if a child is placed with the prospective adopter, especially if the child encounters discrimination or exclusion ... the child may face rejection if they have behavioural problems. Is the prospective adopter aware of this and how would they cope and support the child?

If childless prospective adopters are expecting to take on an older child, they are likely to have less contact with other parents. Opportunities to start building social support networks often occur when meeting other parents while collecting children from nursery or primary school. As children generally become less dependent with age, there may be fewer social interactions between different families. The practitioner may need to consider how well equipped such a prospective adopter is to forge relationships with others in their local community.

ASSESSOR'S ANALYSIS

- Does the applicant have a support network which includes local, practical support as well as emotional support?

- Is there evidence that people in their support network have been used in the past and are willing to be called upon in the future?

- Is there anyone within their network who could be a "back-up carer" in the event of an emergency or unforeseen circumstances? If so, what actions have been taken to explore and develop this?

- If there is someone who will have significant involvement in the care of a child, is there a need to include them in the assessment?

- Where there are gaps in the support network, how could these be filled? Is there evidence that the applicants are able to make new relationships where this is anticipated?

- Are the applicants prepared and willing to use support from social workers and other professionals as needed by the child?

- Are there any implications for the adoption support plan?

> **Verify through:**
>
> - **Personal references**
>
> - **Interviews with key people in the network (if not referees)**
>
> - **Additional written references where appropriate**

Accommodation

A health and safety check should be completed with the applicants and included in C9 of the PAR. DCSF Guidance also suggests use of the Home Inventory.

- Can you describe your accommodation and garden (if applicable) and how long you have lived here?

- Is your home privately owned or rented? If rented, how secure is the tenancy and is the landlord aware of your plan to adopt?

- Is your home suitable for children? Are there any alterations or adaptations you would need to make?

- Will a child placed have their own bedroom and, if not, what arrangements would there be and how would this impact on the child or any other children in the family?

- Have you any plans to renovate or alter the property in any way?

- Have you any plans to move house in the future? Have you considered the implications of this for a child placed for adoption?

DCSF Practice Guidance on Preparing and Assessing Prospective Adopters

The assessment should consider the physical environment where a child will be placed, its size, layout and location. Whether a child will expect to have their own bedroom will depend on their background and this will need to be considered during the matching. Nevertheless, prospective adopters should be able to show an understanding of why a child's need for space will be related to their history and how they might help a child to settle into a different home environment.

Prospective adopters should be encouraged to look at how the living, sleeping and playing spaces may need to change to meet the child's needs. This may affect others in the family and how they plan for and manage these changes may provide insights into their capacity to cope with change.

The practitioner should establish who owns the home and, if a couple are applying, what this information indicates about the stability and permanence of their relationship. If it is rented, is the tenancy secure and is it in joint names? If the prospective adopters are owner-occupiers, is the mortgage in joint names? Where only one of them owns the home, this may be because one partner moved into a home already owned by the other. It would be relevant to ask whether they understand the legal and financial consequences, whether both are equally happy with their arrangement or whether they have any plans to change it.

Access to local services/neighbourhood and community

- Can you describe your neighbourhood?

- In what ways is it suitable for children?

- Are there any potential risks or dangers for children? If there are, how can these be minimised?

- Describe the town, village or area that you live in.

- What resources and amenities does it have that would benefit children (e.g. schools, health, leisure)? Where are they located?

- If any of these are not within your own community, where can they be found and what transport is available?

- Are there any known risks or dangers in the local community?

- In what ways have you been involved in, or contributed to, your local community?

- How easy is access to other areas of the region?

ASSESSOR'S ANALYSIS

- **In your opinion, is the accommodation suitable for a child to be placed in terms of size, layout, furnishings, décor, hygiene, play space, etc, and in terms of security of tenure?**

- **Are you satisfied that the rent or mortgage is being paid and there is no risk to the applicant's living situation through eviction or repossession?**

- **What does the local neighbourhood have available which would benefit a child being placed?**

- **What enquiries has the applicant made about health, education and children's services support systems that are likely to be available to them after placement?**

- **Indicate the applicant's willingness to seek professional help, should this become necessary, after the child is adopted.**

- **Are all the necessary amenities and resources within easy reach or is transport available to access them?**

- **To what extent is the applicant integrated into or isolated from their local community?**

Verify through:

- **Health and safety check**

- **Assessor's observations of local area**

- **Any referees who live locally**

Financial circumstances

A financial statement should be completed with the applicants with evidence seen of bank or mortgage statement, wage slips, etc. This is then recorded in Section A.

- How would you describe your present financial situation?

- Is your present accommodation position financially secure?

- Do you have any debts? If so, how are you managing these?

- What is your general attitude towards money? How do you manage your finances?

- If a couple, do you have different attitudes towards money and financial management?

- Have you made any preparation for the impact that adopting a child will have on your financial situation?

- If you are planning to change your working arrangements when a child is placed with you for adoption, what financial adjustments will you need to make?

- Are you aware of any benefits, including adoption statutory pay, that you may be entitled to?

- Do you have any plans over the next few years to make any major changes, such as in employment or moving house, which would impact on your financial situation?

DCSF Practice Guidance on Preparing and Assessing Prospective Adopters

The key issue for their assessment is whether the prospective adopter can meet the needs of a child placed for adoption with them, whatever their income level.

So rather than looking only at the amount of income, questions the practitioner should explore are whether the prospective adopter's income and benefits, if any, are likely to be sufficient to meet the family's needs before and after adoption... and how well the family budget is managed. Do they live within their means or do they have substantial debts?

As income and expenditure may be a source of conflict in relationships, where couples are being assessed, the practitioner should try to understand how they manage and decide their spending. In some cases, the way any disagreements are decided could provide the practitioner with an insight into the stability and permanence of their relationship.

ASSESSOR'S ANALYSIS

- Does the applicant's general financial situation appear to be secure?

- If they have any debts, is there evidence that these are being managed/repaid and will not create any difficulties for the applicant?

- Do they need any further assistance in identifying benefits, allowances they may be entitled to or eligible for?

- Have they planned for any necessary financial adjustments when a child is placed with them and for any future needs?

Verify through:

- Checking pay slips, bank statements, reference from mortgage company or landlord

- Reference from an accountant if self-employed

Motivation

- How long have you been thinking about adopting a child?

- What was your initial motivation for adopting a child?

- Why do you feel now is the right time for you to adopt?

- (If a couple) Has this been a difficult "journey" for each of you and how have you supported each other through this?

- Have you involved other people in your decision to adopt?

- What do you feel you can offer a child placed with you for adoption?

- What age and number of children do you feel would fit best in your family ?

- Do you know anyone else who has adopted or who has been adopted?

- What made you approach this adoption agency to assess you as adopters?

Childless applicants

- What is the reason for you not having or not being able to have children of your own?

- If you have made a conscious decision not to have birth children, what are the circumstances that led to this and are you both equally agreed on this decision?

- What support have you given each other? Have you received support from family and friends?

- Are you aware that some feelings about not having birth children may arise again in the future at different times? How would you deal with these feelings?

- (For lesbian or gay applicants) Have you considered any other routes to becoming parents e.g. surrogacy, donor fertility treatment? If yes, how have you coped with any disappointments and when did you decide that adoption was the right route for you?

Childlessness through infertility

- How and when was your infertility discovered? How did you react to and deal with this at the time?

- What support did you give to each other? Did you receive support from anyone else?

- Were you offered or did you seek any counselling?

- What treatment have you received and when did your last treatment finish? Ask the applicants to draw a timeline which shows their journey to conceiving a child. Any treatments, pregnancies, miscarriages, death of a child? When, how, what was the impact of each event? How did you deal with this individually and as a couple?

- How did you reach the decision to stop any treatment you were having?

- What has been the process for you of coming to terms with not having a child of your own? Why do you feel now is the right time to adopt?

- Do you still take any contraception to prevent pregnancy? Are you prepared to do this if you are approved to adopt/matched with a child? (This question can be adapted to reflect the agency's policy.)

- Are you aware that some feelings around infertility may arise again in the future at different times? How would you deal with these feelings?

Applicants with a birth child/ren

- What has led you to decide to add to your family through adoption?

- Do you plan to have more children of your own in the future and, if so, when and how many?

- What do you feel are the issues that might be raised by having both birth children and adopted children in your family?

ASSESSOR'S ANALYSIS

- **Does the applicant's motivation to adopt seem to be well considered, realistic and based on an understanding of the lifelong nature of adoption?**

- **Where a couple is applying to adopt, do you have a clear understanding of their "journey" to reaching the decision to adopt and do you believe that they are equally committed to adoption?**

- **Where the applicant has experienced infertility, do you have evidence of how the applicant experienced their infertility and processed the subsequent pain and disappointment?**

- **Do you have a sense of any particular vulnerabilities which the applicant might have as a result of their infertility? Are there any specific support needs stemming from their experience of infertility?**

- **Is there evidence that the applicant has come to terms with the issues of loss raised through infertility whilst recognising that they may experience feelings of loss being triggered after a child is placed?**

- **Can you demonstrate what the applicant has learned about the issues raised in adoption during the preparation assessment process and how this has impacted on their application?**

Verify through:

- **Medical references**

- **Personal references**

- **Personal statement by applicant/s**

Understanding and expectations about children and the lifelong nature and impact of adoption

- What do you think might be the differences between being a parent to birth children and being an adoptive parent?

- What research / reading have you done since deciding to adopt?

- What do you know about the experiences children may have had which lead them to need to be placed for adoption?

- Are there any background situations that you would be concerned about e.g. parent with mental health, alcohol or drug misuse, learning disability? How would you deal with limited or unreliable information available on the child and their family background?

- How might you expect an adopted child to react to being separated from their parents, siblings or other significant people, e.g. foster carers?

- What do you think are the effects of loss and poor attachment upon children?

- How might you expect a child who has experienced neglect, physical or sexual abuse in the past to behave in your home?

- If a child has not had a good experience of attachment to their parents, how might this affect them? What could you do to help them form positive attachments to you?

- Can you understand how some children being placed for adoption are "stuck" in their development and may act younger than their actual age? How might you be able to help such a child?

- Do you understand that behavioural difficulties can continue and/or recur over longer periods of time? Can you give examples of possible scenarios?

- What sort of behaviours would you find the most difficult?

- How do you think you will respond to a child rejecting you?

- If you have been able to meet with experienced adopters, what have you learned from them?

Sexual abuse

- What do you see as the dilemmas involved in caring for a child who may have been sexually abused? Is this a background factor you feel able to consider?

- Is there any overtly sexual behaviour you do not feel able to deal with?

- If applicable, what do you think are the implications for such behaviour on other children within your family and network and how would you manage this?

- Do you have any reservations about parenting a child born from an incestuous relationship?

Health issues

- Do you feel able to parent a child with health issues? Are there some illnesses or conditions you would find difficult to manage? What support do you think you may need with issues such as uncertainty about a child's future, acceptance, bereavement and confidentiality?

- What experience do you have of managing health issues with children or other adults that you could draw on?

Physical/learning disabilities

- Do you feel able to parent a child with a physical disability? If so, what specific needs do you feel able to meet?

- Is your accommodation suitable or will you require help to adapt it?

- What local resources are available?

- Could you parent a child with learning difficulties? What level of disability would you be able to manage?

- Would you expect the child to be able to move on to independent living? What do you understand to be the implications of caring for a child who may not achieve independent living?

- What understanding do you have of the sexual needs of a young person with physical impairment/learning disabilities?

Puberty/adolescence

- What do you think are the extra dilemmas associated with parenting adopted teenagers?

- What are your views on emerging sexual development or sexual experimentation?

- How would you ensure appropriate sex education?

- How do you envisage supporting an adolescent who is lesbian/gay?

- What is your attitude to children/young people experimenting with alcohol, drugs and smoking? What dilemmas or difficulties do you think this will pose for you?

Telling and contact

- Do you understand the importance of telling a child placed with you at different ages and stages of development, that they were adopted? Have you thought about how to do this?

- How would you share with a child what is known of their history and the circumstances that led to them being adopted by you? What support might you need?

- How would you keep the child's knowledge of their birth family up to date and relevant to their circumstances?

- How do you feel about meeting a child's parent/s for a one off meeting? What do you understand to be the benefits of this for you and the child?

- What do you understand about the importance of maintaining some contact with the birth family of a child placed with you?

- What level of contact do you feel you could support with different family members if it was important to the child? Do you expect that this might change over time?

- Have you had any involvement with contact arrangements as a child or a parent, which could help you understand and deal with the emotional and practical implications of this?

- During adolescence there are many challenges but we are increasingly aware of adopted children using social networking sites to make contact with members of their birth family. Have you thought about how you might make them aware of the risks involved in this?

- When your adopted child becomes 18, they will be entitled to see their adoption records and could decide to make contact with birth family members. How would you prepare them for this before they reach 18?

DCSF Practice Guidance on Preparing and Assessing Prospective Adopters

Children with a history of attachment disorder or difficulties, neglect or abuse pose particular difficulties for their carers. Such children may fail to recognise hazards and dangers. Their dysfunctional attachment behaviour may initiate inappropriate responses to strangers that could in turn lead to inappropriate relationships with adults or other children. Their raised anxiety levels may trigger unexpected episodes of deep distress or aggression that prospective adopters may find difficult to comprehend and cope with.

The capacity of prospective adopters to ensure the safety of such children is a key factor to be assessed. These include helping the prospective adopter understand that a child exposed to prolonged neglect or abuse is likely to continue to behave in a way that may provoke distress, feelings of rejection or anger in others.

The prospective adopter's views on contact are an essential part of their assessment and these should be explored. Many prospective adopters are uncertain and ambivalent about contact. Prospective adopters should be made aware that the child's adoption plan will specify the proposed contact arrangements and that these are based on the child's assessed needs.

ASSESSOR'S ANALYSIS

- How realistic is the applicant in their understanding of the needs of children being placed for adoption?

- Are they realistic about the types of background situations and current circumstances of children they wish to consider?

- How much preparation or research have they undertaken?

- Are there gaps in their knowledge and experience and how could these be filled?

- Have they shown an understanding of the importance of "open communicativeness" in relation to a child's birth family?

- Will they be able to facilitate and work with any contact plans for a child placed with them?

- Will they be open in talking to a child about being adopted?

Previous adoption or fostering experience

Information about previous applications can provide valuable evidence of parenting but equally, any failed applications should be fully explored and documented.

- Have you, or any member of your household, previously applied to become a foster carer, adopter or childminder?

- If so, who, when, where and what was the outcome?

- If you were approved, what has your experience been and what do you bring from that experience to this application to adopt?

- If you have previously adopted a child, have you used any adoption support services?

- If you were not approved, you withdrew, resigned or were deregistered, what were the events that led to that situation?

- Were any complaints or allegations made about you, and if so, what were the circumstances and how were they resolved?

ASSESSOR'S ANALYSIS

- **Have any previous experiences of adoption or fostering been verified through references from the approving agency?**

- **How can any previous experience benefit this application? Are there any support or training needs highlighted by any previous experience?**

Verify through:

- **References from local authority checks and any other identified agencies**

- **Information from previous files/records**

- **Ofsted references and report if registered as a childminder**

Experience of caring for children

- Thinking of your own experience of being parented, what would you change and what would you repeat as a parent yourself?

- As a couple, did you have different experiences of being parented? How will you agree on how you will parent together?

- (Where couples come from different ethnic backgrounds) Do you feel there were differences in how you were parented which impact on your views of parenting and how have you resolved these?

- What experience do you have of looking after children, either professionally, as a parent or looking after other people's children?

- What are your strengths in caring for children and can you give examples of these?

- Are there any areas which you find difficult and what support might you need?

- How would you manage the differing needs if you have siblings placed with you (where applicable)?

- Can you give examples of how you have managed children's behaviour? How do you/would you encourage positive behaviour?

- What are your views on corporal punishment?(Worker to explain agency's policy) What punishments would you use for children depending on their ages?

- What is your understanding of why play, hobbies and activities are important for children? How would you encourage these with a child placed with you?

- How would you build up a child's self-esteem and make them more resilient?

- Some children's behaviour can put them at risk of harm. How would you keep children safe? Can you give examples of this?

- How do you encourage children to make decisions and learn from mistakes?

- Do you feel children confide in you? Can you give an example? Are there any examples of when you have helped children cope with big changes in their lives and how did you do this?

- What do you see as your role as parents in encouraging and supporting your adopted child's education?

- What has been your experience of contact with other organisations which may be involved with a child placed with you (i.e. school, GP, therapist)?

For applicants who already have birth or adopted children

- What does being a parent mean to you?

- How did you adjust to becoming a parent?

- What do you think have been your biggest challenges as a parent and how have you dealt with these?

- What do you think have been your biggest rewards as a parent?

- What do you see as your strengths and weaknesses as a parent?

- If a couple, are there particular parenting roles that you each take?

- How will you balance meeting the needs of the children already in your family with a child/ren being placed with you?

- What difficulties do you anticipate and how will you manage these?

DCSF Practice Guidance on Preparing and Assessing Prospective Adopters

Most prospective adopters will have views about how they were helped or not helped to play, learn and develop at home as children. Exploring the opportunities the prospective adopter was offered by their parents to play and learn is usually an easy way to start this discussion.

Practitioners should also discuss with the prospective adopter their understanding of child development and the help and support children might need at different stages of development. It should also be made clear that some children had little stimulation in their earlier home lives and may be functioning well below their chronological age.

Where prospective adopters already have children, observation of how they relate to them provides a helpful basis for discussion.

ASSESSOR'S ANALYSIS

- How realistic is the applicant about what is involved in becoming an adoptive parent?

- How much preparation or research have they undertaken?

- Have they been able to show an understanding of the physical, emotional and psychological needs of children being placed for adoption?

- Is there evidence of their experience or potential to manage the behaviour of an adopted child in an appropriate way?

- Is there evidence that the applicant has been successful in parenting their own children? How might this transfer to their plan to adopt a child?

- What experience have they had with other people's children and what have they learnt from this that they could bring to parenting an adopted child?

- Is there evidence that the applicant would promote and support a child's health and education?

- Are there any gaps in their experience, skills or knowledge and if so, how could these be filled?

- What do you see as their strengths as parents?

- Do you have any concerns about their parenting?

Verify through:

- **Personal references**
- **Previous partners**
- **Previous employers (if work involved children)**
- **Interview with any birth or adopted children**
- **Interview with any adult children and children from previous relationships**
- **References from schools or health visitors**
- **Feedback from preparation and any further training undertaken**
- **Evidence of reading any books/articles about adoption**
- **Personal references**

Promoting the child's cultural heritage and religious beliefs

- What do you understand as a person's "identity"?

- Why is it important to care for an adopted child in a way that maintains a positive sense of their identity?

- What experience do you have of challenging discrimination towards yourself or others? How do you respond to this?

- If you are considering adopting a child from a black or minority ethnic background or from a different country, what issues in relation to their identity and self image do you envisage they might have to deal with? How would you envisage addressing this with them?

- How would you help a child deal with racism or discrimination of any kind?

- If you are considering adopting a disabled child, how would you promote a positive sense of identity for them?

- How would you feel if your adopted child disclosed that they were gay or lesbian? Is there anyone in your family or support network who might find this difficult?

- Do you understand that children may come from backgrounds where their own families held and expressed discriminatory views and they may have absorbed some or all of these attitudes and values? How would you deal with this?

- How could you help a child develop a positive view of Britain as a multiracial/ multicultural society?

ASSESSOR'S ANALYSIS

- Does the applicant present an open minded attitude and an understanding of Britain as a multiracial, multicultural country?

- Does the applicant understand the importance of promoting a child's heritage and culture and have ideas on how to do this?

- Where relevant, how would a child from a different ethnicity feel living in this family and area?

- How would the applicant deal with their adopted child disclosing that they were gay or lesbian?

- Do you feel the applicant could meet the needs and promote the development of children whose background is different to their own e.g. ethnicity, religion, culture?

- Are there people in their support network who would be a valuable resource to them?

- Have training or support issues been identified?

Verify through:

- **Personal references**

- **Feedback from preparation training**

- **Support network**

Anticipated changes in the applicant's life and lifestyle

- Describe a typical weekend in your household.

- Describe your routine during the week.

- How will having a child placed with you impact on the lifestyle of individual family and household members?

- Who does what in the family and are gender roles important to you?

- What are the written or unwritten "rules" that exist in your household or that you would introduce for a child being placed?

- What is your attitude to food (i.e. healthy *v* convenient/fast food)? How would you manage a child who had difficulties with food?

- What leisure activities do you and any other family members enjoy individually and as a family?

- Do you have a computer and access to the internet? What rules are in place or would you introduce when a child is placed?

- What role do religious/cultural practices play in your household? How would this change when a child is placed with you?

- How do you celebrate special occasions (birthdays/religious festivals/Christmas/anniversaries)?

- What kind of holidays do you enjoy? How might this change when a child is placed?

- (Where there are other children in the family) How is affection displayed between family members? How do you deal with people's feelings in your family? Do family members pick up on how others are feeling? Do you encourage discussion? Can you think of any examples?

- If there are going to be any changes in your work situation once a child is placed, have you thought about the impact of this on you? If you are continuing to work, how will you manage the arrangements that you will be putting in place to provide child care for the child?

DCSF Practice Guidance on Preparing and Assessing Prospective Adopters

Most prospective adopters enjoy writing an account of "a day in their life" and knowing that the adoption panel will see it should help motivate them. The practitioner may use their account to obtain a clearer picture of the individual and their current family functioning.

Although not an in-depth analysis, it is likely to contain useful information about their culture, lifestyle, friendships and their peer group that can lead into discussion about the social functioning of the family a child may join.

ASSESSOR'S ANALYSIS

- **What evidence is there that the prospective adopters have thought about the changes there will be to their lifestyle when a child is placed?**

- **How flexible or rigid are they with regard to current routines and how these may change?**

- **Are any additional childcare arrangements that will be put in place agreed as being appropriate to the needs of a child being placed for adoption?**

- **How "child friendly" is the household at present and what thought have they given to changing this?**

- **What evidence is there that this is a family that deals appropriately with feelings and emotions?**

> **Verify through:**
>
> - **A written exercise on a day or week in the life of the applicants**
> - **Personal references**
> - **Interviews with any children in the household**

Contribution of the applicant's wider family and support network

Some questions relating to this are covered in the *Social and support network* section.

- Do you understand what adoption support will be offered by the agency?
- What is your understanding of how to access it and what do you anticipate using?
- (If a couple) In the event of a breakdown of your relationship, what would you do to limit the impact on your adopted child?
- What is your understanding of the possibility of a disruption occurring and what can be done to try and avoid these situations by the agency and adopters?

Expectations about the child/ren that they hope to adopt

- What age, sex, number of children are you hoping to adopt?
- How have you come to this view? Have your thoughts changed during the assessment period?
- How would this fit into your current family situation?
- Could you consider a child with a learning or physical disability? If so, to what degree and why?
- Could you consider a child with health issues? If so, to what degree and why?
- Are there types of behaviour that you would feel unable or unsure of managing (i.e. attachment difficulties, aggressive behaviour, sexualised behaviour)? If so, why?

NB: This area of questioning should only be used to rule out any clear areas where the applicant should not/does not want to be considered as their views may change following training or during the matching process.

ASSESSOR'S ANALYSIS

- **Is the applicant being realistic about the age, sex and number of children that they want to adopt? Is there any difference of view between you?**

- **Are they being realistic about the type of behaviours they could manage?**

- **What are the adoption support implications, including financial?**

- **What evidence, where relevant, is there that they could care for a child with a disability?**

Verify through:

- **Personal references**

- **Interview with members of the family/household**

- **Support network**

Potential testamentary guardians

- Who would you choose to be a testamentary guardian for a child placed with you in the event of your death? Have you discussed this with them?

- What are your reasons for choosing this person?

- What financial arrangements would you make to support this arrangement?

Analysis, evaluation and summary of key factors leading to the recommendation

- Summarise the strengths and positives of the application.

- Set out any vulnerabilities that have been identified in the assessment and any plan for how these could be addressed through training or support.

- Acknowledge any differences of views between the applicant and the assessing social worker.

- Be clear about what information has been evidenced and what is the worker's professional opinion.

DCSF Practice Guidance on Preparing and Assessing Prospective Adopters

In completing the report, the practitioner should ensure (the report) provides an analysis of the information within the report and a clear indication of whether or not the prospective adopter is considered suitable to adopt a child.

It should make clear distinctions between facts, opinion or conjecture and it should set out the evidence for the strengths and weaknesses of the prospective adopter.

Personal reference visit

- How long have you known the applicants?

- In what capacity do you know them?

- How frequently do you have contact with them now or in the past?

- How would you describe each of the applicants (i.e. personality, temperament, etc)?

- What do you feel they will bring to parenting an adopted child (i.e. patience, flexibility, resilience, sense of humour, etc)?

- Do you consider their relationship to be a stable one?

- Do they support each other?

- For single applicants, where do they get their support?

- If the applicants have children of their own, how would you describe them?

- Do you have any comments or observations as to the way they have brought up their own children?

- Do you have any comments or observations about how the applicants relate to other people's children?

- Are the applicants tolerant of people who are different for reasons of disability, ethnicity, religion or sexuality?

- Have you seen them under stress for any reason and, if so, how have they managed this?

- Are there any areas where you might envisage they may experience difficulties or need support?

- Do you have any concerns about their emotional or physical care of a child placed with them?

- Do you believe that the child will be safe from any type of abuse?

- What understanding or experience do you have of adoption or fostering and the issues involved in adoption a child?

- What discussions have you had with the applicants about the following issues:

  - Whether they will be able to talk to a child about being adopted and the reasons for them being adopted?

  - Whether they will support any form of contact with birth family members, e.g. parents or siblings by letter or face to face?

Issues for social workers

NB: Agencies may want to consider providing a copy of the write up of this visit to the referee asking them to agree the content. This would not need to include the assessing social worker's analysis of the information obtained, but gives confirmation that their views have been accurately represented.

Where the referee has raised concerns about the application or where the information given by them creates concern for the worker, it is important that there is discussion about whether and how the information can then be discussed with the applicant.

DCSF Practice Guidance makes it clear that 'if the referee raises serious concerns about the prospective adopter, or the relationship if they are a couple, these should be carefully considered by the agency. Where the concerns remain, the prospective adopter should be given an opportunity to respond.' However, the agency should not disclose the specific source of the concerns to the prospective adopter either directly or in the prospective adopter's report, which they will see. Referees should be assured in writing and during the interview that the agency will not disclose this information to the prospective adopter unless they request it and the referee consents to its disclosure. Otherwise, they will be very unlikely to provide information which could be central to the questions the agency needs to answer.

At the end of the reference, the assessing social worker should indicate what weight they would place on this reference based on the length and strength of the relationship with the applicant and the referees' understanding of the issues presented by adoption.

Health and safety checklist

Below is a sample checklist which will help you look at issues of health and safety in the applicant's home. It is very likely that your agency will already have such a checklist.

Kitchen

- Is the chest freezer kept locked?

- Are kettle flexes short?

- Are knives safely stored?

- Are surfaces kept clean?

- Is the fridge clean?

- Does the fridge have a thermometer and safety lock?

- Is there a cooker guard?

- Are cleaning materials stored safely?

- Is there a fire blanket?

- Are pets allowed in the kitchen?

- Where do pets eat their food?

Living areas

- Are rooms clean and in good decorative order?

- Is flooring clean and safe?

- Is furniture in good order?

- Does furniture conform to BSS safety standards?

- Is there sufficient heating?

- Are there any glass tables, etc, that could be a potential hazard?

- Are large areas of glass of the safety variety or are they covered with safety film?

- Is a fire guard required?

- Are there/will there be socket covers where young children are being placed?

- Are DVDs/videos for adult viewing stored out of view and reach?

Hallway/stairs/landing area

- Is flooring safe and in good condition?

- Are the stairs safe?

- Are banisters filled or do they have a maximum gap of four inches?

- Is the lighting sufficient?

- Are smoke detectors fitted and working at each level of the house?

- Are stair guards required?

- Is the area clear of clutter or any fire hazards?

- Where is the key to the front door kept?

Any bedrooms to be used for child/ren

- Are childproof locks fitted to the windows?

- Is the room light and airy?

- Is the room in good decorative order?

- Is the flooring clean and safe?

- Is the heating sufficient for the room and fixed to the wall?

- Is there a suitable bed and bedding?

- Is there suitable storage space for the child's belongings?

Bathroom

- Is the bathroom clean and hygienic?

- Are facilities sufficient for the proposed number of occupants of the house?

- Is there a suitable lock on the door that could be opened in case of emergency but out of reach of young children?

- Is the light or any heater operated by a pull cord?

- Are shampoos and cosmetics stored out of reach?

- Are razor blades and any electrical devices stored safely?

Cars/garage

- Are all vehicles taxed up to date? On what date was the tax disc seen?

- Are all vehicles covered by comprehensive insurance? On what date were the certificates seen?

- Do all vehicles have an up-to-date MOT? On what date were the certificates seen?

- Are all vehicles fitted with suitable safety restraints?

- Are the applicants aware of the regulations regarding the safe carrying of children?

- Do they have/will they obtain car sets that comply with safety standards?

- Are any potentially hazardous DIY fluids safely stored?

- Is all DIY equipment safely stored?

- Is there a chest freezer in the garage? Is it lockable?

- Is the garage kept locked?

Garden

- Is all gardening equipment stored safely in a locked shed?

- Is the back garden securely fenced in?

- Is any play equipment safe and securely attached?

- If there is a trampoline, does it have a safety net?

- Is any sandpit clean and hygienic?

- Is there a cover for any rotary washing line?

- Are any garden ponds safely covered or securely fenced in?

- Are there ponds or hazards in neighbouring gardens that might pose a risk?

- Is the applicant aware of any dangerous plants which should be removed?

- Is any greenhouse fitted with safety glass and kept locked?

- Is the garden kept clear of pet waste?

- If there is a swimming pool or hot tub, is it kept safely covered?

General

- Is alcohol stored safely and out of reach?

- Are cigarettes, lighters and matches stored out of reach?

- Is the applicant a non smoker (if child being placed is under 5)? If a smoker, where do they smoke? Are there any issues arising from this?

- Are gas appliances and boiler serviced annually? On what date were the safety certificates seen?

- Is there a fire extinguisher?

- Is there a fire escape plan?

- Are medicines stored safely and securely?

- Is there a first aid box with suitable and in-date contents?

- Do any toys in the home appear clean and safe and comply with safety standards?

- If the applicant has guns in the house, are they securely stored and does the applicant have a licence which has been checked?

- Do any pets appear safe, friendly and hygienically cared for?

- Is there adequate house insurance and buildings and contents insurance? On what date were the certificates seen?

- Where applicants live on a farm, there should be particular attention paid to safety in relation to machinery, outbuildings, accessibility to farm land, and contact with farm animals.

ASSESSOR'S ANALYSIS

- **A final section should identify clearly what needs attention prior to any child being placed.**

Pet ownership questionnaire

- This questionnaire should be completed when any type of pet is kept in the household. Where there are several pets, more than one form may need to be completed.

1 What type of pets do you keep?

Dogs	Cats	Small Mammals	Birds	Reptiles	Insects	Other
☐	☐	☐	☐	☐	☐	☐

2 Breed and number of pets? Where the breed of dog is registered under the Dangerous Dogs Act 1991 (amended 1997), the social worker should discuss this with their manager as a matter of priority. For further guidance, see BAAF Practice Note 42 *Placing Children with Dog-Owning Families*.

3 Size of pet(s)?

Small	Medium	Large
☐	☐	☐

4 Age of pet(s)?

5 What training has your pet(s) received?

6 Who trained the pet(s)?

7 Qualification of trainer?

8 Where are the pet(s) allowed in the house?

Kitchen	Living room	Dining room
☐	☐	☐

Master bedroom	Small bedrooms	Other
☐	☐	☐

9 What area is exclusive (if any) to the pet(s)?

Caged compound	Garden	Other: Specify
☐	☐	☐

10a Where do the pet(s) sleep at night?

b Where do the pet(s) sleep during the day?

11 Temperament of the pet(s)?

Boisterous	Usually placid	Playful	Possessive
☐	☐	☐	☐
Nervous	Docile/submissive	Protective of persons	Protective of property
☐	☐	☐	☐

12 Where does the pet(s) go to the toilet? Who takes responsibility for clearing this up?

13 If you are a breeder of pets, where does this take place?

14 What happens to any offspring, where are they kept?

15 Has the pet(s) ever bitten or hurt anyone?

Yes	No
☐	☐

If yes, what treatment was needed?

16 What contact/experience has the pet(s) had of children staying overnight at the house?

17 Where is the pet fed? Can food be removed from the pet safely?

18 Where is the pet normally exercised?

19 Who normally exercises the pet?

20 Is the pet registered with a vet? Does it have vaccinations, worming treatment/flea treatment as needed?

21 When present pet(s) die, do you intend to replace it/them?

Yes   No

☐   ☐

22 How would you recognise conflict between the pet and child/infant?

23 If there was conflict, which of the following would you do?

Take the pet to an agency   Pet to friend/relative

☐   ☐

Put the pet down   Request the removal of the child

☐   ☐

24 Any other information you consider to be relevant

Adapted with kind permission from Solihull Metropolitan Borough Council.

Safer caring

It is important that any policy or advice on safe caring for adopters recognises the differences in adoption placements where the child is being established as a family member from policies relating to foster carers. However, the following areas would benefit from discussion.

Areas to discuss

- Showing affection in a way that builds attachments but also protects the child and adopters
- Use of physical punishment or restraint
- Maintaining privacy in the home e.g. dressing appropriately
- Washing, bath time and bedtime routines
- Supervising children within the home (to include use of computers and mobile phones)
- Monitoring children outside the home
- Managing allegations
- Keeping adoption records secure
- Ensuring safety of friends and family network

Example of an ecomap

Below is an example of a completed ecomap. Guidance on drawing an ecomap is also available in Form F.

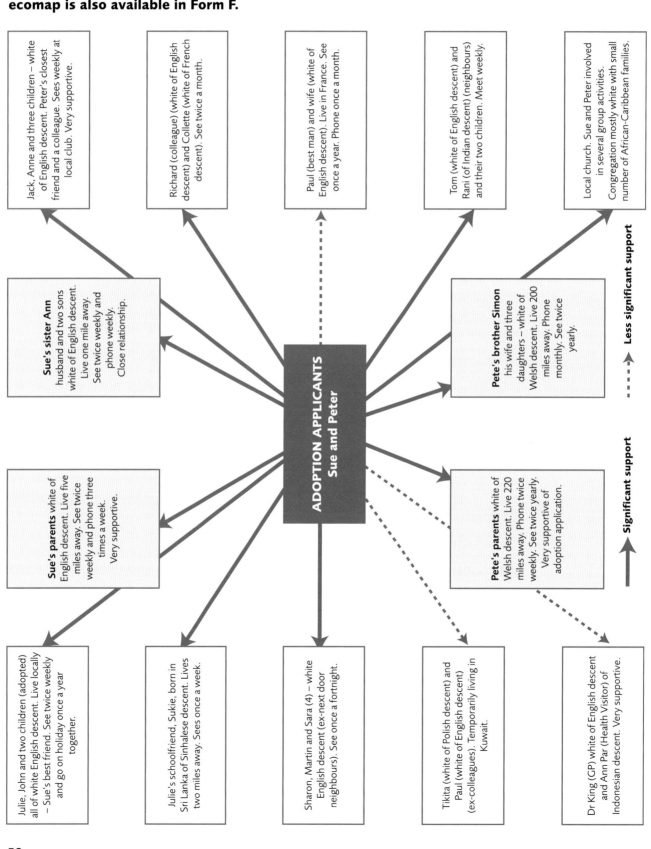

Appendix 1

Adoption assessment time sheet

Name of applicant/s...

Subject covered	Completion date
Family of origin	
Other significant relationships/previous relationships	
Identity	
Education/employment	
Health/leisure	
Other relevant information – Criminal checks	
Current adult relationship	
The household and its membership	
Social and support network	
Accommodation/neighbourhood/community	
Financial circumstances	
Motivation	
Understanding and expectations about children and the lifelong nature and impact of adoption	
Previous applications	
Experience of caring for children	
Promoting child's cultural and religious heritage	
Current and future lifestyle	
Support once child placed	
Placement considerations	
Identification of Testamentary Guardian	

Appendix 2

Additional areas to cover for adoption of specific child by foster carers or relative carers or intercountry adoption applications

Adoption of specific child by foster carers or relative carers

- Do the applicants understand the differences in the role they would be taking on as an adoptive parent rather than a foster carer/other relative in relation to the child?

- What is their motivation to adopt this child? Are they feeling / being put under any pressure by the child, their social worker or other family members to make their application?

- Do the applicants understand the lifelong implications of adoption e.g. responsibility into adulthood, supporting further education, inheritance implications?

- Have they discussed with their children the implications for their inheritance? What views have been expressed about this?

- What impact will adopting this child have on any other individual members of the family?

- Are there any issues relating to existing contact arrangements or birth parents having knowledge of the carers or where they live? (Although these are matching considerations, they should have been considered by the prospective adopters in making their application.)

Intercountry adoption applications (Some of these questions are adapted from BAAF Form F3)[1]

- Explore the applicant's reasons for seeking to adopt a child from overseas, whether domestic adoption was explored and how the choice was made if applicable.

- Outline each applicant's familiarity with and knowledge of the country concerned and how has this been gained and whether they have existing links with the country or how they intend to build links? What attempts has the applicant made to develop links with families from the child's country of residence living in the UK? Do they already have friends who share the child's ethnic origin?

- What are the attitudes or views of the extended family members on the applicant's plan to adopt a child from overseas and any implications for the applicants or child placed?

- How does each partner view the ethnicity and culture of the other? What is each applicant's understanding of Britain as a "multiracial/multicultural" society? How is this reflected/demonstrated in their present lifestyle?

- What does this family understand about the impact upon children of discrimination and racism? Does each applicant understand and promote an anti-racist approach to parenting? How is this (or will this be) demonstrated?

- How will they help a black/minority ethnic child cope with racism?

- How will each applicant help their adopted child establish herself/himself as a young person in the UK where her/his peer group might be drawn from diverse other communities as well?

- How have existing children been involved in discussion about the implications of adopting a child from overseas and what are their views and understanding of the impact on them?

- If the adopters have previously adopted from overseas, have they discussed how this adoption may differ to their previous experience? How will they deal with any differences in this application e.g. different country, different background circumstances?

- Does the applicant have resources to finance the intercountry adoption process and meet the financial commitment of bringing up an adopted child without recourse to public funds?

- Outline each applicant's understanding of the reasons for children being made available for adoption in the country concerned and how these may impact on the needs of the children, including the implications of pre-birth experiences, early deprivation, abandonment and experience of institutional care. What is their understanding of the position or experiences of the birth parents?

---

[1] BAAF Form F3 is still used by some agencies for intercountry applicants. BAAF is currently working with the Intercountry Adoption Centre to develop a PAR for intercountry adoption applications.

- What is their understanding of, and attitude towards, the likely pre-placement experiences of the child and the implications of the child's background, particularly when coming from institutional care, on the potential for bonding with the applicant? Outline the applicant's understanding of techniques to promote attachment, and proposals to assist the bonding process when the child is placed with the applicant.

- What plans do the applicants have to assist the language development of a verbal, non English-speaking child? What is the attitude of each applicant towards attempting to learn some of the child's first language?

- What strengths and experience does this family have to help them parent a child whose culture, religion, ethnic origin and/or language are different from their own? What changes do they anticipate making in their lifestyle in order to enable them to do this and to what extent will they embrace the child's culture and country of origin?

- What plans does the applicant have with regard to the following issues:

  - keeping the child's culture alive

  - meeting the child's spiritual needs

  - developing the child's ability to communicate in his/her language of heritage

  - helping the child feel a sense of belonging to, and pride in his/her cultural heritage

  - visiting the child's country of origin after the adoption order is made

- How will the applicants manage any reactions from their immediate circle of friends and the wider community to them becoming a transracial/transcultural family? How will they deal with experiences of racism encountered by themselves or the child? What strategies do they envisage using?

- How will the applicant manage the period of introductions and caring for the child whilst in the country of origin? Have they considered the possible sense of isolation and the additional need for support during this time for them and any existing children who remain at home? What changes do they envisage to their lifestyle?

- Does the applicant have contact with other families in the UK who have adopted a child from the same country? How will the applicant maintain these links?

- What medical conditions and/or risks could the applicant consider, including where the child's health history may not be known or where the child may have related disfiguring facial characteristics due to lack of early medical treatment and what is their capacity to care for a child whose hepatitis or HIV status is uncertain?

- To what extent has the family considered the possibility of the child having serious learning/behavioural difficulties? For applicants considering a child with physical or learning difficulties, outline the nature and severity of difficulty considered appropriate for the applicant, and the special skills/experience of each applicant in caring for such children. Has each applicant visited or had contact with adults with similar special needs to those that they are prepared to consider in their adopted child? How does the applicant propose to meet the needs of this adopted child in adulthood?

Appendix 3

Brief Prospective Adopter's Reports

The Adoption Agencies Regulations (AAR)2005 25 (7) which came into force on 30 December 2005 included provision for the preparation of a brief Prospective Adopter's Report in relation to the prospective adopter's suitability to adopt.

Once an application to adopt has been accepted and an assessment has been started, if the agency then has concerns about the prospective adopter's suitability to adopt based on information they receive during the assessment process and decide not to complete the assessment or a full PAR, they should visit the applicants and advise them of their concerns. If the applicant does not wish to withdraw their application, then a brief report must be prepared. The brief report is then considered by the agency's adoption panel and subsequently the agency's decision-maker and can lead to a "qualifying determination" which gives prospective adopters the option of applying to the Independent Review Mechanism (IRM) or making representations to their adoption agency.

It is important, therefore, that the brief PAR provides enough evidence to show why prospective adopters are not suitable to adopt and therefore should not have a full assessment and PAR completed.

The *DCSF Practice Guidance on Preparing and Assessing Adopters* sets out that:

> *Where the agency forms the view during the assessment process that the prospective adopter may not be suitable to adopt, the practitioner may prepare a brief prospective adopter's report. This could be where, for example, the practitioner comes across significant information during the assessment, or evidence emerges from the health report, local authority report, or report of the interviews with referees. When a brief prospective adopter's report is prepared, the prospective adopter should be counselled, and the brief report sent to the prospective adopter before being submitted to the adoption panel.*

The overview report on the IRM[1] published by the former DCSF in 2009 highlighted some areas of concern about these reports.

---

[1] http://www.dcsf.gov.uk/everychildmatters/_download/?id=6603

It highlighted that:

- there were concerns about the length and detail provided in the reports with some reports being completed after a lengthy assessment but not reflecting all the information gathered;

- some assessments did not reflect the strengths of the applicants alongside the concerns;

- greater analysis was often needed of information obtained during the assessment;

- reports did not always provided a balanced and up-to-date picture of the applicants based on the information gathered;

- second opinion visits were not commonly used with brief PARs whilst recognising that statutory guidance is not clear about whether they are required in these applications.

It is good practice for the following information to be included in a brief report. This could be presented within the format of the PAR with a clear indication of where work has not yet been undertaken on each section due to the decision to complete a brief report or in a separate report format as decided by the adoption agency.

- The date an application was accepted, details of the number of visits undertaken and the date the report was prepared.

- All statutory checks undertaken, including CRB, medicals and personal and professional references and their outcomes, with an analysis of any concerns that arise from these checks.

- Written accounts of any reference visits undertaken with an evaluation of the information provided. These may provide helpful evidence to support your recommendation or may offer another view of the applicants which needs to be recorded to provide balance.

- NB: In a brief report, issues may have arisen primarily related to third party information from references. Thought will need to be given to how this information is presented within the report if it has been given as confidential information and a request has been made not to disclose this to the applicants. Advice may need to be sought from the agency's legal adviser on this issue.

- Full details of all the information gathered during the assessment to date.

- A summary of the issues which have raised concerns and how these have been discussed with the prospective adopters. It is important that a distinction is made between information that is evidenced and the social worker's professional opinion.

- Any response from the prospective adopters together with any supporting evidence offered by them should be included with the brief report.

- Analysis of the strengths and concerns raised by the assessment setting out clear reasons for reaching the conclusion that a recommendation is made that the applicants are not suitable to adopt.

- Although not required by legislation, a second opinion visit should be undertaken to provide another view of the concerns being raised. Where this takes place, a report on the visit with analysis of the information provided and a recommendation on suitability should be included with the brief report and seen by the applicants.

Appendix 4

Second opinion visits

There is no specific reference to second opinion reports in the Adoption Agencies Regulations. They are introduced in *Statutory Guidance* Chapter 3 (48) which states that:

> *The social worker who assesses the prospective adopter should draft the report for the adoption panel, highlighting any issues of concern, and submit it to his or her team manager. The manager should arrange for another team manager or another adoption social worker to visit the prospective adopter to discuss any issues of concern or where clarification is needed. A visit by another social worker provides the opportunity for securing a second opinion on the prospective adopter and their assessment before the report to the panel is finalised.*

Some adoption agencies have been routinely completing a second opinion report on all assessments presented to their adoption panels whilst others have introduced them, for cases where there are concerns, since December 2005.

Second opinion reports are a useful part of the assessment process. They provide an opportunity for:

- a different and objective perspective on the assessment which may result in new issues or information being shared;

- obtaining the applicant's view of the process and their relationship with the agency;

- checking and reporting on areas of concern or those that need clarification and to provide any additional details needed;

- the applicant to reflect on how their views have developed in relation to all aspects of adoption;

- reinforcing both the strengths and areas for development of the applicant and identifying any issues that may be focused on at the adoption panel.

Preparation for the visit

Prior to the second opinion report visit, the PAR should be completed by the assessing social worker and have been seen by applicants with the opportunity for them to comment on the report.

Where the applicants are from a black or minority ethnic background not reflected by the assessing worker, consideration could be given to a black worker being involved in the second opinion report.

The person undertaking the second opinion visit should not have been involved in management of the case. They should read the report and discuss with the report writer any issues they feel would benefit from further discussion as well as identifying any areas that they wish to explore.

Areas to be covered during the visit

- How applicants have found the preparation and assessment process
- How the applicants feel they have developed during the assessment and training
- Pertinent areas from the PAR, e.g.:
    - motivation
    - resolution of infertility
    - issues arising from family background
    - impact of how the applicant was parented and/or their ideas of parenting
    - support networks
    - any issues raised by referees which have been shared with the applicants
    - any issues raised from statutory checks
    - expectations of children
    - ability to deal with difficult behaviours
    - impact of placement on lifestyle
    - impact on other children in family and their views of placement (children would not be seen during second opinion visit)
- Confirm ages and number of children being considered

Content of report

The report should contain the following.

- Brief summary of impressions of the applicants
- The development of the applicants during the assessment period
- The areas from the PAR that were covered during the visit
- Strengths and any concerns or areas identified for support
- Recommendation on suitability by second opinion worker

NB: If significant concerns are raised during this visit or new information emerges, the assessing worker may need to undertake a further piece of work to address this and complete an addendum to the PAR to deal with these issues.

The second opinion report should then be made available to the applicant in the same way as the PAR for comment and signature.